Doreen Rappaport

The Boston Coffee Party

Pictures by Emily Arnold McCully

SCHOLASTIC INC.

New York   Toronto   London   Auckland   Sydney
Mexico City   New Delhi   Hong Kong   Buenos Aires

For Alexandra and Gretchen

ISBN 0-439-38486-9

Text copyright © 1988 by Doreen Rappaport.
Illustrations copyright © 1988 by Emily Arnold McCully.
All rights reserved. Published by Scholastic Inc., 555 Broadway, New York, NY 10012, by arrangement with HarperCollins Publishers.
SCHOLASTIC and associated logos are trademarks and/or registered trademarks of Scholastic Inc.

12 11 10 9 8 7 6 5 4   5 6 7/0

Printed in the U.S.A.   23

First Scholastic printing, January 2002

Contents

1 · Sugar, Please

Emma popped a handful of berries into her mouth.

"Stop eating those berries," said her sister, Sarah.

"We need them for jam."

Mrs. Homans opened the cupboard.
"The sugar jar is almost empty,"
she said.

"Run to the store and
get some sugar, Sarah.
And take your sister with you
before she eats all the berries."

"Let's go to

Merchant Smith's shop,"

said Emma.

"All right," said Sarah.

"Good morning, Merchant Smith,"

said Sarah.

"Do you have sugar?"

"Sorry, no sugar,"

said Merchant Smith.

"With the war going on,

getting sugar is hard."

"Do you have any sugar?"
Sarah asked at the next shop.
"Sorry. All sold out,"
said Merchant Forbes.
"With the war going on,
getting sugar is hard."

Emma and Sarah walked

from shop to shop.

The answer was the same everywhere.

They walked to the last shop.

"This is Merchant Thomas's shop.

Mother told us

not to buy from him.

He charges too much,"

said Emma.

"But we need sugar

or the berries will spoil,"

said Sarah.

She walked into the shop.

Emma walked in after her.

"Do you have sugar?" asked Sarah.

"I have five pounds left,"
said Merchant Thomas.

"I will take it," said Sarah.

"Seven shillings a pound,"
said Merchant Thomas.

"But everyone else charges
five shillings," said Sarah.

"Everyone else
does not have sugar.
If you think it costs too much,
do not buy it,"
said Merchant Thomas.

"We will buy it," said Sarah.

She put the money on the counter.

17

Just then the door opened.

"Good morning, Mrs. Arnold,"

said Merchant Thomas.

"Do you have sugar?"

asked Mrs. Arnold.

"Yes, eight shillings a pound,"

said Merchant Thomas.

"I will take it," said Mrs. Arnold.

"That is *our* sugar," said Sarah.

"I did not take your money yet.

So you have not bought the sugar,"

snapped Merchant Thomas.

"That is not fair," cried Emma.

But Merchant Thomas

was not listening.

He poured the sugar

into a sack for Mrs. Arnold.

"You are so greedy,"

shouted Sarah.

She picked up the money
and ran out of the shop.

Emma ran after her.

When Sarah told her mother
what had happened,
her mother's face turned red.
"We can do without jam," she said.
"But one day Merchant Thomas
will be sorry."

"May I eat the berries then?"

asked Emma.

Mrs. Homans smiled.

"Go ahead," she said.

Emma popped some berries

into her mouth.

2 · The Sewing Party

Emma looked around the room.

Everyone was busy making shirts.

Emma's mother was cutting patterns.

Mrs. Smith was sewing sleeves.

Sarah was sewing on buttons.

Emma put down her needle.

"I finished the hem, Sarah.

What should I do next?"

"Sew a message into the shirt,"

said Sarah.

"Then the soldier who gets it

will know who made it."

"What shall I say?" asked Emma.

"Anything you want," said Sarah.

Emma thought.

Then Emma picked up her needle
and sewed
HELLO from EMMA
"If Papa gets your shirt,
he will be very happy,"
said Sarah.
"I hope the war ends soon.
Then Papa will come home,"
said Emma.
"I miss Papa so much."
"Me, too," said Sarah.

Mrs. Homans banged her scissors on the table.

"Ladies, I have something to say."

The women looked up.

"First, the good news,"

said Mrs. Homans.

"We have finished

over two hundred shirts."

The women smiled at one another.

"What is the bad news?"

asked Mrs. Smith.

"Merchant Thomas is selling sugar

for eight shillings a pound,"

said Mrs. Homans.

"Everyone else charges five."

"What a greedy man,"

said Mrs. Smith.

"We must tell everyone

not to buy from him,"

said Mrs. Homans.

Just then the door opened.

It was Aunt Harriet.

She looked angry.

"Do you know what
Merchant Thomas has done?"
she cried.

"He has locked up
forty barrels of coffee
in his warehouse."

"But why?" asked Mrs. Smith.

"He is waiting until

no one in Boston has coffee,"

said Aunt Harriet.

"Then he will sell his coffee

for a lot of money."

"He is greedier than I thought,"

said Mrs. Homans.

"We must teach him a lesson,"

said Aunt Harriet.

"But what can we do?"

asked Mrs. Smith.

The room was quiet.

"Let's have a party!"

Sarah shouted suddenly.

"Silly girl,

this is no time for a party,"

said Mrs. Homans.

"I mean a party

like the men had

when they threw English tea

into the harbor,"

said Sarah.

"What a fine idea,"

said Aunt Harriet.

"Yes," said Mrs. Homans.

Everyone agreed.

Mrs. Homans stood up.

"Let's meet tomorrow morning

at eight o'clock at Corn Hill,"

she said.

"Invite all your friends.

Tell them to bring

wagons and carts

and pots and pans

and cups.

We are going to have

a coffee party!"

3 · Pots and Pans and Cups

"Wake up, Emma," said Sarah.

"But the sun is still asleep,"
said Emma.

"Never mind the sun," said Sarah.

"We must do our chores
before we can go
to the coffee party."

Emma dressed quickly

and ran to the barn.

Sarah was milking the cow.

"Hurry up," Emma told the chickens,
as she reached for their eggs.

Mrs. Homans poked her head
into the barn.

"Are you ready?" she asked.

"Ready!" Emma and Sarah shouted.

Corn Hill was packed
with women and children,
pushing wagons and carts
and carrying pots and pans and cups.

"Good morning, ladies,"

said Mrs. Homans.

"Are you ready?"

"Ready!" the women shouted.

They walked toward

Merchant Thomas's shop.

He was sweeping his sidewalk.

"Good morning, Merchant Thomas,"

said Mrs. Homans.

Merchant Thomas looked at

the women and children

and wagons and carts

and pots and pans

and cups.

"Good morning, ladies," he said.

"What can I do for you?"

Mrs. Homans stepped forward.

"We need coffee for a party."

"I am sorry," said Merchant Thomas.

"I do not have coffee."

"That is not true," said Aunt Harriet.

"You have coffee in your warehouse."

"*That* coffee is not for sale,"

said Merchant Thomas.

"Why not?" asked Mrs. Smith.

"None of your business!"

"It *is* our business,"

said Aunt Harriet.

"Give us the key to your warehouse,"

said Mrs. Homans.

"I will not!"

Merchant Thomas said.

"Yes, you will," said Mrs. Homans.

She pushed him into the cart.

Mrs. Homans and Aunt Harriet

started pushing the cart.

"What are you doing?"

Merchant Thomas shouted.

They pushed the cart

faster and faster and faster.

It bumped down

the cobblestone streets.

"Put me down!"

shouted Merchant Thomas.

"Give us the key and we will,"

shouted Aunt Harriet.

"Never!" Merchant Thomas shouted.

Aunt Harriet and Mrs. Homans

pushed the cart even faster.

Merchant Thomas bounced up and down.

His feet flew up in the air.

Aunt Harriet and Mrs. Homans
pulled the cart to a sudden stop.
Merchant Thomas fell out of the cart.
"The key!" Aunt Harriet shouted.

"Here," said Merchant Thomas.

He handed the key to Aunt Harriet.

"Thank you, sir," she said.

"Follow me," cried Mrs. Homans.

The women raced to the warehouse.

Aunt Harriet turned the key

in the heavy wooden door.

"Look at all those barrels,"

cried Emma.

One by one,

the women rolled the barrels

out the door.

Then they took off the lids
and scooped out the coffee beans.
They rolled the empty barrels
back into the warehouse.

Aunt Harriet locked the door.

Then the women and children

pushed their wagons and carts

and pots and pans

and cups of coffee home.

"You will be sorry,"

Merchant Thomas shouted after them.

"Not as sorry as you will be
when our men return from the war,"
cried Mrs. Homans,
hugging her daughters.

Author's Note

This story is based on a true incident.

From the 1760s on, many colonists, angry at high taxes imposed on some British goods, decided not to buy them. During the Revolutionary War, women met in large groups to spin, weave, and sew shirts for the rebel soldiers. They formed committees and asked merchants to hold down prices on sugar and coffee. Most merchants agreed, but Abigail Adams wrote her husband John about what happened to one wealthy merchant who hoarded coffee:

A number of females, some say a hundred, some say more, assembled with a cart and trunks, marched down to the warehouse, and demanded the keys, which [the merchant] refused to deliver. [One woman] seized him by his neck, and tossed him into the cart. Upon his finding no quarter, he delivered the keys, when they tipped up the cart and discharged him; then opened the warehouse, hoisted out the coffee themselves, put it into trunks, and drove off.